What Do I Do When ...

I'M SCARED!

Danielle Haynes

PowerKiDS press

PK Beginners

I'm scared!
I want to hide.

I went to the store with Dad. I can't find him!

I don't know what to do! I want to cry.

Who can help me?

My dad says everyone feels scared sometimes. It's OK.

Even grownups get scared sometimes!

My mom says the
best thing to do
is ask for help.

I call for Mom or Dad
when I hear a noise
at night.

I ask the police for help when I'm lost.

OLICE
MINNEAPOLIS
CITY OF LAKES
POLICE
A. SANCHEZ

My teacher can also make me feel safe.

Feeling scared is OK. And now I know what to do!

Published in 2026 by The Rosen Publishing Group, Inc.
2544 Clinton Street, Buffalo, NY 14224

First Edition

Editor: Danielle Haynes
Book Design: Jeffrey Taylor

Photo Credits: Cover Prostock-studio/Shutterstock.com; p. 3 Paul Vasarhelyi/Shutterstock.com; pp. 5, 7 Andrew Angelov/Shutterstock.com; p. 9 Krakenimages.com/Shutterstock.com; pp. 11, 15 fizkes/Shutterstock.com; p. 13 La Famiglia/Shutterstock.com; p. 17 Media_Photos/Shutterstock.com; p. 19 Nic Neufeld/Shutterstock.com; p. 21 Drazen Zigic/Shutterstock.com; p. 23 Robert Kneschke/Shutterstock.com.

Cataloging-in-Publication Data
Names: Haynes, Danielle.
Title: I'm scared! / Danielle Haynes.
Description: Buffalo, New York : PowerKids Press, 2026. | Series: What do I do when...
Identifiers: ISBN 9781499455984 (pbk.) | ISBN 9781499455991 (library bound) | ISBN 9781499456004 (ebook)
Subjects: LCSH: Fear in children--Juvenile literature. | Fear--Juvenile literature. | Emotions in children--Juvenile literature.
Classification: LCC BF723.F4 H39 2026 | DDC 155.41246--dc23

Manufactured in China

CPSIA Compliance Information: Batch #QWPK26. For further information contact Rosen Publishing at 1-800-237-9932.